Kids Can Do It!

I CAN START A BUSINESS!

by Ruth Owen

WINDMILL
BOOKS

Published in 2018 by **Windmill Books**, an Imprint of Rosen Publishing
29 East 21st Street, New York, NY 10010

Produced for Rosen by Ruth Owen Books
Designer: Emma Randall

Photo Credits: Courtesy of Ruby Tuesday Books and Shutterstock.

Cataloging-in-Publication Data
Names: Owen, Ruth.
Title: I can start a business! / Ruth Owen.
Description: New York : Windmill Books, 2018. | Series: Kids can do it! | Includes index.
Identifiers: ISBN 9781499483543 (pbk.) | ISBN 9781499483482 (library bound)
  | ISBN 9781499483376 (6 pack)
Subjects: LCSH: New business enterprises--Juvenile literature. | Entrepreneurship--
  Juvenile literature. | Small business--Management--Juvenile literature.
Classification: LCC HD62.5 O94 2018 | DDC 658.1'1--dc23

Manufactured in the United States of America
CPSIA Compliance Information: Batch BS17WM: For Further Information contact Rosen Publishing, New York, New York at 1-800-237-9932

WARNING:

Some of the activities in this book require adult help.
It's also important that all laws and regulations are followed when
carrying out the activities in this book. The author and publisher disclaim
any liability in connection with the use of the information in this book.

CONTENTS

BECOME AN ENTREPRENEUR

Would you like to have more money to spend on books, music, games, or new clothes? Are you saving for a big purchase such as a new bike or TV?

If the answer is yes, maybe now is the time to become an **entrepreneur** and start your own business!

Running a business will help you discover what you like doing and what you're good at.

You'll learn new things, gain confidence, and have fun.

You won't just earn money, you'll learn how to manage money, too.

Becoming a young entrepreneur might even give you ideas for your future after school.

There's always plenty of yard work to be done. Why not get paid to do it?

What Is Business?

Business is all about producing a product or providing a service and earning money in return.

SELLERS AND BUYERS

You might not realize it, but you already take part in business as a customer.

Let's say you buy a particular **brand** of candy. *Why do you choose that brand?*

Maybe it's because you like the taste better than other brands. The company that makes the candy probably spent a lot of time experimenting with different flavors to get the taste just right.

Maybe the TV commercial appealed to you because it shows people your age enjoying the candy and having a good time. The company wanted someone like you to buy their product, so they promoted it in a way that attracted you.

Maybe the candy is cheaper than other brands. When a company has lots of competition, it may give its product a price that's lower than other brands to attract customers.

You've experienced business as a customer. Now it's time to be on the other side of the transaction by attracting, supplying, and pleasing customers of your own.

YOUR BIG IDEA

The first step in starting a business is to have an idea. Your idea might be connected to your hobby or favorite pastime.

Maybe your business idea helps to satisfy a need or solve a problem. For example:

Problem: Your aunt does not have a babysitter for your little cousin during the school holidays. She works from home and needs help taking care of her boisterous little boy.

Your business idea: Offer your services as a babysitter so your aunt can quietly get on with some work.

Once you have an idea, it's time to do some **market research**.

Business idea

Growing sunflowers to sell in pots.

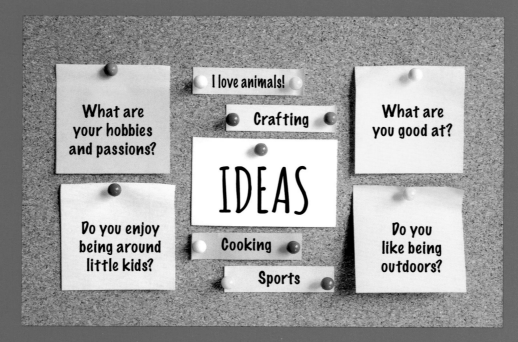

MARKET RESEARCH

Is there a need for your product or service?

Who is your target customer?

Are there other businesses in your area offering the same service or product?

How much do they charge?

How good is the competition, and what could you do differently?

Business idea

Designing and making clothes and costumes for dogs.

Maybe your business idea is car washing. How can you beat the competition?

Business opportunity: Every Saturday, your neighbor takes his car to the car wash. The price to wash the car in the automatic system is $10.00.

Your business idea: You offer to wash the car in your neighbor's driveway for $5.00. Your service is cheaper, and your neighbor doesn't even have to leave his house. You're in business!

Business idea

Washing cars.

KNOW YOUR BUSINESS MATH

Ever wondered how you'll use math in the real world? When you start a business, you'll be doing math all the time.

Once you have an idea for your business, it's time to think about **start-up costs**. For example, if you're starting a baking business, do you need to buy equipment?

To pay the start-up costs, you'll need money known as **capital**. You might have savings or birthday money to use. Perhaps a relative will lend you the money.

A person might **invest** in your business to make some money. For example, the **investor** lends you $50.00. In return, you agree to pay back the $50.00 plus **interest** of $2.50. You get the capital you need, and in return for taking a risk and helping you get started, the investor earns money.

In order for a business to be successful, it must make money.

A **profit** is the difference between your sales (money taken from customers) and your expenses (money you spend to operate your business). If expenses are higher than your sales, you'll make a **loss**.

EXAMPLE A

Make a batch of 20 cupcakes
Ingredients $7.50
New mixing bowl $5.00
Total expenses $12.50

Sell 20 cupcakes at 50¢ each
Total sales $10.00

Your expenses were greater than your sales, so you've made a loss of $2.50.

EXAMPLE B

Make a batch of 20 cupcakes
Ingredients $7.50
New mixing bowl $5.00
Total expenses $12.50

Sell 20 cupcakes at $1 each
Total sales $20.00

You have made a profit of $7.50.

How will you use your profits?

You can repay your investors.

You can use the profits to build your business. For example, you could buy some cookie cutters so you can sell cupcakes and cookies.

You can spend or save them.

Your expenses, the prices you charge, and the number of sales you make all affect how much profit your business makes.

SPREAD THE WORD

In order to find customers, you will need to advertise and promote your business.

Everything to do with promoting your business is called **marketing**.

1 Tell your friends and family about your new business and ask them to spread the word.

2 Make a poster to promote your business. Check with an adult that they are happy with the information you've included on the poster.

You can draw a poster with markers, and then make copies.

You can design and print your poster using a computer.

Display your poster in windows or on bulletin boards in places such as your local community center, grocery store, or other places of business. Always ask permission before putting up a poster.

Need help mowing your lawn?

Then you need

KIDS CAN DO IT MOWING SERVICES

• Reliable • Hardworking
• Competitive prices

Tel: 111 222 3333

3 Use a computer to turn your poster into a leaflet. Deliver the leaflets to homes around your neighborhood. Always go leafleting with an adult or a friend.

You can fit six leaflets on one sheet of printer paper.

Print out or make lots of copies.

IT'S ALL ABOUT TEAMWORK

It's possible to promote your new business online using social media. You can also set up and design your own website. When using the Internet to promote your business, ALWAYS ask an adult to help you.

4 One of the best advertisements for your business is word-of-mouth. Do a good job for your customers and they will tell other people!

Re: Rainbow cake

Dear Ellie
Everyone loved the rainbow cake you baked for the party. I've passed on your name to two friends who want to order cakes....

YOUR BUSINESS PLAN

It's great to have a plan! Before you start work on your big idea, try answering these 10 questions. Your answers will form a business plan.

My Business Plan

1. Why am I starting this business? What are my goals?

2. What is my product or service?

3. Who is my target customer?

4. What competition do I have?

5. What price is my product or service?

6. How will I market my business?

7. What equipment do I need and what are my start-up costs?

8. How much capital do I need and where will it come from?

9. How much profit do I hope to make this summer, in my first year, or other period of time?

And finally . . .

10. What is my business called?

STAY SAFE

When running your business, it's essential that you stay safe. Discuss your business idea with the adults who take care of you. Before you start work, make some rules together and stick to them. For example:

You will discuss all your business plans together.

If you're working away from home, you'll take a friend or trusted adult along.

You will always give your trusted adults the name, address, and telephone number of your customers.

You will text or call regularly if away from home to say you are OK.

You will agree on a time to be home, and stick to it.

IT'S ALL ABOUT TEAMWORK

Ask an adult to help you contact your local government offices to find out if there are any **regulations** controlling businesses in your area. For example, are you old enough to do the work you want to do? Do you need a **permit** to sell food or other products? Make sure you know the rules and then follow them!

MUD CAN MEAN MONEY! CAR WASHING

You may already be bursting with ideas for your new business. If not, on the following pages we've put together a selection of fun ways that you can become a young entrepreneur.

JACK & JEN'S

CAR WASH

Small cars $5.00   Large cars and SUVs $10.00

Every Saturday

We come to you!

To schedule an appointment call 111 222 3333

If you enjoy being outdoors and physically active, car washing could be the business for you.

Ask relatives and friends if they'd like their cars cleaned. You can also market your business to neighbors by leafleting nearby streets.

You could run your business from your family's driveway. Or, with friends for help and safety, you could go to your customers' homes or workplaces.

Before you start a business, you can test out your products or services on potential customers.

Ask friends or relatives if you can clean their car for free.

Once you've finished the job, ask them for honest **feedback**. How many points out of 10 would they give you for your service? This is called a **focus test**.

If your score is low, ask them what they think you could do differently. If the score is high, you're ready to charge for your services.

Getting some practice will help you improve your skills, and you can time how long it takes to clean one car. This will help you figure out how much to charge.

To start your business, you'll need access to a hose and some basic equipment.

Cleaning cloths

Sponge

Car soap

Bucket

GET EARNING WITH YARD WORK

Do you sometimes help out at home by cutting the grass? If so, you have the skills and experience to turn this into a business.

Many people can't mow their lawns, or don't have time to do it. Some people might need help if they're taking a long vacation.

Start a grass-mowing business, and you could be earning money all summer!

IT'S ALL ABOUT TEAMWORK

The start-up costs for this business could be high if you need to buy your own lawnmower. Ask an adult to help you buy a secondhand mower. Then learn how to safely use it with some adult supervision. You might also need an adult to drive you and your mower to your jobs.

There are lots of other jobs to be done in yards and gardens.

In the summer, customers might need their plants watered when they are on vacation. In the fall, you could make money raking up leaves.

Customers might need help pulling weeds from paths, sidewalks, patios, or driveways. You don't have to be a plant expert to do this. If it's growing on the path, the customer wants it gone!

Weeds

IT'S ALL ABOUT TEAMWORK

Most banks offer savings accounts for people under 18 that you can manage jointly with an adult. Once your business makes a profit, you can deposit this money in your account and watch your savings grow.

CUSTOMERS THAT WOOF!

If you're a dog lover, a dog-walking business could be just right for you!

Dogs need to be walked every day. So once you have a four-legged customer, you'll be earning money all year round.

It's possible to walk two dogs at once if they get along. Then you'll be earning double the money, and the dogs will enjoy having a canine companion.

Get started by asking friends and family if they need help with their dogs. Elderly neighbors might also be very pleased to get some help.

Once you have a customer, visit to meet with the dog and ask these questions:

The downside to this business is that you'll need to pick up the dog's poop. Your doggie customers will also still need their walk when it's freezing cold or pouring rain.

How far or for how long should the dog walk?

Is there a particular place you should walk the dog? (Make sure you only walk in busy parks or on busy streets.)

Is the dog friendly to other dogs?

Is the dog afraid of anything?

START A PET-SITTING BUSINESS

Another great way to earn money as an animal lover is as a pet sitter.

When pet owners are away from home, they often need someone to feed and check in on their pet.

To do this work, you'll need to be very responsible. The animal will be totally relying on you, and you'll have a key to your customer's home.

As a pet sitter you might carry out the following tasks:

Feed the pet.

Give the animal fresh water.

To advertise your dog-walking or pet-sitting business, you can make posters. Then, with permission, put up your posters on bulletin boards at your local veterinary offices and pet food stores.

Spend some time petting and playing with the animal.

Water potted plants.

Take in mail and newspapers.

BECOME A PARENTS' HELPER

If you enjoy helping out with younger brothers or sisters, spending time with little kids could be the business for you.

You may not be old enough or feel ready to care for a young child on your own. However, you could become a parents' helper.

During school vacations or on weekends, parents may be working from home or have chores to do around the house. While your customers get on with their work, you keep their children entertained.

In time, once you're older and more experienced, your business could become a babysitting service. Then you will stay home alone with a baby or young child.

IT'S ALL ABOUT TEAMWORK

The American Red Cross runs babysitting courses for 11- to 15-year-olds. The classes teach you how to deal with medical emergencies. They also teach you how to care for and entertain young children, and how to handle difficult behavior. It's possible to take one of these courses online.

GET CREATIVE

Be a successful parents' helper by preparing lots of activities for the children in advance. Always be sure that your customers know what you have planned, and that they will be in the house so you and their kids will be safe.

Visit the library and borrow books to share with the children.

Little kids love new things to play with. So take along some of your old toys, but make sure they are age-appropriate.

Ask your customers if you can build an indoor fort. You'll need a table and a couple of sheets. Then you and the children can camp out inside the house.

Quilts and cushions

Take along some strings of battery-powered lights.

With your customers' permission and guidance, plan a nature treasure hunt in the backyard. Write a list of things to find. For example:

An orange leaf

A smooth stone

A puddle

A worm

A cobweb

Before you finish for the day, always pick up and put away the toys and clear away any activities. Your customers will be impressed by your **professionalism**.

A NAIL ART BUSINESS

If you and your friends have fun creating funky nail designs, turn your creativity into a nail art business.

Go online and watch YouTube tutorials to improve your nail art techniques and learn new skills. Beauty magazines also contain lots of ideas and tips.

When you feel ready, ask your mom, older sister, aunts, and friends to spread the word about your business.

As soon as you start a business, begin keeping **accounts**. Your accounts are a record of the sales you make and your expenses, such as paper for leaflets and nail polish. You can write your accounts in a notebook, or set up a **spreadsheet** on a computer.

COME TO A PARTY!

Ask an older friend or relative to host a nail art party and invite three or four friends.

You will then be paid to paint each guest's nails and create some cool designs with nail art stickers.

You will need:

- Nail polish remover and cotton pads
- A nail file
- Nail clippers
- A selection of nail polishes
- A selection of nail art stickers
- Tweezers for handling the stickers
- A top coat

A quick guide to funky nail art:

- Remove any old nail polish.
- Clip or file the nails, as needed.
- Paint on a base coat of colored nail polish.
- Carefully add a sticker to each nail.
- Paint on a clear top coat.

MAKE MONEY WITH YOUR CREATIVITY

If you enjoy art, crafts, or design, start a business selling unique items made by you!

If photography is your thing, turn your photos into beautiful greeting cards.

1 Choose your favorite pictures. If you wish, you can use computer programs to add effects.

2 Many online stationery companies offer a service printing greeting cards. Upload your photos, and follow the instructions to turn them into cards.

3 Wait a few days, and the cards will be mailed to your home.

Printing cards in this way can cost around 50 cents per card. This means you can sell them for $1 and make a healthy profit!

IT'S ALL ABOUT TEAMWORK

Many people who make craft items sell them online through websites such as eBay and Etsy. If you're under 18, you can jointly set up an account with a trusted adult. Also, ask an adult to help you research craft fairs and markets in your local area where you might be able to sell your work.

T-SHIRT DESIGN BUSINESS

If drawing or painting is your thing, use your talents to create custom painted T-shirts.

Babies, toddlers, teens, adults – almost everyone wears tees, so you have a lot of target customers.

1 Buy plain T-shirts online or from stores for just a few dollars.

2 Buy fabric paint from an art and crafts store. There are hundreds of different colors to choose from, including glitter paints.

3 Paint your designs onto the T-shirts. Finally, follow any instructions on the paint containers to make your design permanent.

Give your friends free T-shirts to wear. When someone asks, "Where did you get that shirt?" your friends can tell the potential customer about your business.

SWEET TREATS FOR SALE!

Cupcakes, cookies, pumpkin pie, gingerbread – if you love to bake treats like these, why not try earning some money from your skills?

There's a huge amount of competition, but start small and market your products to the people you know.

For example, if everyone loves your pumpkin swirl brownies, send a photo by email in early October. Tell your friends and family that you're taking orders for Halloween and Thanksgiving.

Everyone loves home-baked treats, but not everyone has time to make them!

Draw or use a computer to create a logo for your business. This is a unique name, symbol, or design that customers will recognize.

Ruby's Bakery

We love cakes as much as you!

Show off your baking skills by giving away free samples.

For example, ask Mom to take some of your cakes into her office. Make sure she hands out leaflets, too.

Try passing around some of your home-baked cookies at your younger sibling's soccer game.

Tips for your baking business:

Make sure it will be OK to use your family kitchen as your workplace.

Always clean up after a baking session.

Research cake prices in stores and at markets and bake sales.

Check out new trends online, in magazines, and on TV shows. Cupcakes and macaroons have both been popular in recent times. What's the next big thing?

If you love animals AND baking, why not produce home-baked dog treats? Make sure your products are healthy and nutritious by following recipes from a dog treat recipe book that's been written by experts.

Home-baked dog biscuit

Doggie cupcake

I CAN START A BUSINESS!

Starting a business is something that many adults don't even do. So if you can bring your business idea to life, you have every reason to feel proud!

Hopefully, your business will make a profit and be successful.

Maybe, however, it won't work out, and that's fine, too. Many successful entrepreneurs tried out several different business ideas before they found the one that worked. If you learned new things and had new experiences, you spent your time wisely.

Remember! All business people make mistakes. Learning from your mistakes is also a success!

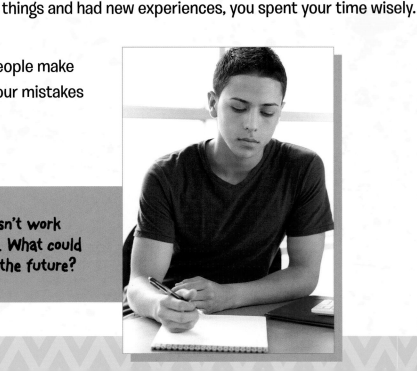

If your business doesn't work out, think about why. What could you do differently in the future?

Your business doesn't have to earn money for you. You can set up a business that donates all its profits to a **charity**. Then, through your hard work, you can help the good causes that are important to you.

Keep trying. You're an entrepreneur, and your next big idea is just around the corner!

Running a business can reward you in lots of different ways, not just with money:

You overcome a challenge

You get respect

You gain knowledge

You have fun

You can feel proud

You gain experience for the future

You learn responsibility

GLOSSARY

accounts
A record of the money that a business spends and receives through sales.

brand
A name, design, symbol, or other feature that helps customers recognize a particular product or service.

capital
An amount of money used to start a business.

charity
An organization that raises money, often from donations, and then uses the money to help the needy or for other good causes.

entrepreneur
A person who sets up a business.

feedback
Helpful information or criticism given to people or businesses to help them improve.

focus test
Testing an idea, product, or service with potential customers to get feedback.

interest
Money paid to a lender in return for a loan. The borrower pays the interest and repays the original sum that was loaned.

invest
Lend money to a business; in return, the investor receives interest or part ownership of the business.

investor
A person who invests in a business.

loss
A financial situation in which a business spends more than it earns in sales.

marketing
Advertising and everything to do with promoting a business to customers.

market research
Gathering information about customers' needs, likes, and dislikes. Also finding out information about competitors.

permit
An official document that gives someone permission to do something.

professionalism
Working or acting in a serious way that shows you have the right skills to do a job.

profit
The money made by a business if its sales are higher than its expenses.

regulations
Rules that are made and enforced by a person or group in authority, such as local government.

spreadsheet
A computer document that is used to record data, such as the accounts of a business.

start-up costs
The cost of buying equipment or materials to start a business.

target customer
A customer who is likely to buy your product or use your service.

WEBSITES

For web resources related to the subject of this book, go to:
www.windmillbooks.com/weblinks and select this book's title.

INDEX